Comes in Waves

Marissa Epler

BookLeaf Publishing

Presentation by *BookLeaf Publishing*

Web: www.bookleafpub.com

E-mail: info@bookleafpub.com

ISBN: 9789357440615

First edition 2023

Peace

The reflections on the water show
Clouds skating by soft, quiet forests
Trees sway side to side with the wind
Mountains overlook the horizon
Silence echoes

Out at Sea

the sound of ocean
its saltiness in my nose
jealousy of land

Cold Nights

I sit at my favorite spot at the top of the hill in
my neighborhood
and watch the leaves fly away and listen to the
trees shake
Shivering in the cold, icicles form around me
As stars appear I count them
One by one
Lights flickcr in windows
And one by one
They're gone

The Luxury

Sometimes I believe,
privacy is a luxury.
A state of being
That knows
I'm not on full display
and nobody's watching.

unfortunate reality

there's only so much we can take
when everything seems the same
there's comfort in the familiar
but when you become numb to it
you'll know
there's something better out there
where you can be a little more free
I want to break out of my skin
let myself heal from the wounds within me
heal from the pain that stings like a burnt tongue

Wanting

what's so funny is
people complicate their lives on purpose
because they believe it will make them
more interesting
but so many people
live fascinating lives
simple
yet so full and whole
it's beautiful to want things
but "that's enough" is beautiful too
to want is to declare something missing
usually the feeling is right
but the thing missing is replaced with something
else
often distracts from the problems
too painful to stare in the face

Lost in Thought

dangling ideas
sometimes get pushed away
by thoughts that float past
on a wave
so some ideas are lost
and forgotten

Nature is Worried About Us

plastic water bottles
fumes of acetone and gasoline
polyester shirts
hyper-sweetened cans of soda
among the
crisp air
drenched in rainfall
fresh fruits of summertime
and earth's scents of soil and worms
dewy grass and perfect sun
looks down on the fakeness we made

To Relax in the Summer

it's shady here
my eyes close gently as a small breeze hits my
nose
soaking up the fresh warm air while it lasts
oh look!
there's someone
I've seen her before
my green cyes glowing in front of her
and soon I walk away
to look for another shaded spot

no more lies

toads and frogs r cool
and if somebody says otherwise
well they are lying to u

Coming of Age

funny how lots your old worries
aren't much like your current ones
now the world is less blurry
and you still try to have fun,
but worries are still there
and they won't go away
so you take more care
to makc yourself feel okay

Shapes We Cannot See

When will clouds
look like animals again?
I don't want to force them
to look like something.
But I miss seeing them.

plain jane

I'm not your plain jane
those two words make me feel
as if I'm slowly fading away
into a caricature of myself.
If you took the time
to know be better,
you'd find I'm multifaceted
And not just there
when you need something pretty to look at.
I'm not your plain jane.

dear someone

dear someone,

hey, it's me
I miss you, and you're missing from me
I want to taste your lips and feel your skin
brush up against mine in a hurry just so we can
feel something, somewhere
but anyway
how was your weekend?
I know we've all been busy
making excuses for people who don't really care
about us
isn't it nice
your eyes hold a steady flame
and the fire overtakes mine
is there any better way to say
I want you more than anything
I wish you could understand that
my mind is racing and all I can think about is the
passion we create
but what happens when it all fades away?

gaze

15

she looks through boxes and finds
pretty film stills of a girl you'd only see in
dreams
like every movement she makes is the right one
not an awkward bone in her body
she fantasizes about what it would be like
to be someone like that

You feel me?

the voice of morning awakes me, takes me by
the hand
said it's time to stop dreaming and go play in the
sand
the feel of warm sunlight, the crunch the leaves
make right under your feet
hugs from your favorite person, car windows to
stick your head out of,
nodding to music and watching planes draw in
the sky.
then comes the taste of day
a drop of lemon and soft tangerine
the sweetness fades too soon and the sour lingers
uncomfortably
but it somehow comforts me
I keep coming back for more

Short Yet Difficult Phase

17

I can sense it
my body slowly aching
my head becomes clouded
with feelings I can't explain
the inflections in people's voices
I can't tell what they mean
I wait for a gush of rage
to bleed out of me
I'm in for a hellish ride

Junk

The man throws junk and screams
But doesn't realize
How loud he gets when the synthetic high
Runs through his bloodstream.
In midair,
he stops.
Sinking into his chair,
He's sorry for what he's done to the poor boy.

Unfazed

19

if i find a rock
and i don't turn it over
i guess we'll never know
what's under there.
some things can just be
left alone

Shopping for Candles

I inhale through my nose
taking in the scent of a candle
with a name that doesn't make sense
It reminds me of tough leather jackets
and expired cigarettes.
Another
is like a campfire
with plenty of marshmallows
I can almost hear
the crackling of firewood
and see embers drifting to the grass.

I Have Hope

I have hope
for a love so wide it bursts
laughter like smoke you cough it up
and a song's verse so true
you'll never stop singing it

www.ingramcontent.com/pod-product-compliance
Lightning Source LLC
Chambersburg PA
CBHW050753180726
48003CB00020B/2555